MOSHI MONSTERS MAD LIBS

concept created by Roger Price & Leonard Stern

PSS!
PRICE STERN SLOAN
An Imprint of Penguin Group (USA) LLC

PRICE STERN SLOAN
Published by the Penguin Group
Penguin Group (USA) LLC, 375 Hudson Street, New York, New York 10014, USA

USA | Canada | UK | Ireland | Australia | New Zealand | India | South Africa | China

penguin.com
A Penguin Random House Company

The publisher does not have any control over and does not assume any
responsibility for author or third-party websites or their content.

Mad Libs format copyright © 2014 by Price Stern Sloan,
an imprint of Penguin Group (USA) LLC. All rights reserved.

© 2014 Mind Candy Ltd. Moshi Monsters is a trademark of Mind Candy Ltd. All rights reserved.

Published by Price Stern Sloan,
a division of Penguin Young Readers Group,
345 Hudson Street, New York, New York 10014.
Printed in the U.S.A.

Penguin supports copyright. Copyright fuels creativity, encourages diverse voices,
promotes free speech, and creates a vibrant culture. Thank you for buying an authorized
edition of this book and for complying with copyright laws by not reproducing, scanning,
or distributing any part of it in any form without permission. You are supporting writers
and allowing Penguin to continue to publish books for every reader.

ISBN 978-0-8431-7608-7

1 3 5 7 9 10 8 6 4 2

PSS! and *MAD LIBS* are registered trademarks of Penguin Group (USA) LLC.

MAD LIBS
INSTRUCTIONS

MAD LIBS® is a game for people who don't like games! It can be played by one, two, three, four, or forty.

• RIDICULOUSLY SIMPLE DIRECTIONS

In this tablet you will find stories containing blank spaces where words are left out. One player, the READER, selects one of these stories. The READER does not tell anyone what the story is about. Instead, he/she asks the other players, the WRITERS, to give him/her words. These words are used to fill in the blank spaces in the story.

• TO PLAY

The READER asks each WRITER in turn to call out a word—an adjective or a noun or whatever the space calls for—and uses them to fill in the blank spaces in the story. The result is a MAD LIBS® game.

When the READER then reads the completed MAD LIBS® game to the other players, they will discover that they have written a story that is fantastic, screamingly funny, shocking, silly, crazy, or just plain dumb—depending upon which words each WRITER called out.

• EXAMPLE (*Before* and *After*)

"_____!" he said _____
    EXCLAMATION   ADVERB

as he jumped into his convertible _____ and
                                                NOUN

drove off with his _____ wife.
                          ADJECTIVE

"*Ouch*_____!" he said *stupidly*_____
    EXCLAMATION   ADVERB

as he jumped into his convertible *cat*_____ and
                                                NOUN

drove off with his *brave*_____ wife.
                          ADJECTIVE

MAD LIBS®
QUICK REVIEW

In case you have forgotten what adjectives, adverbs, nouns, and verbs are, here is a quick review:

An ADJECTIVE describes something or somebody. *Lumpy*, *soft*, *ugly*, *messy*, and *short* are adjectives.

An ADVERB tells how something is done. It modifies a verb and usually ends in "ly." *Modestly*, *stupidly*, *greedily*, and *carefully* are adverbs.

A NOUN is the name of a person, place, or thing. *Sidewalk*, *umbrella*, *bridle*, *bathtub*, and *nose* are nouns.

A VERB is an action word. *Run*, *pitch*, *jump*, and *swim* are verbs. Put the verbs in past tense if the directions say PAST TENSE. *Ran*, *pitched*, *jumped*, and *swam* are verbs in the past tense.

When we ask for A PLACE, we mean any sort of place: a country or city (*Spain*, *Cleveland*) or a room (*bathroom*, *kitchen*).

An EXCLAMATION or SILLY WORD is any sort of funny sound, gasp, grunt, or outcry, like *Wow!*, *Ouch!*, *Whomp!*, *Ick!*, and *Gadzooks!*

When we ask for specific words, like a NUMBER, a COLOR, an ANIMAL, or a PART OF THE BODY, we mean a word that is one of those things, like *seven*, *blue*, *horse*, or *head*.

When we ask for a PLURAL, it means more than one. For example, *cat* pluralized is *cats*.

MAD LIBS® is fun to play with friends, but you can also play it by yourself! To begin with, DO NOT look at the story on the page below. Fill in the blanks on this page with the words called for. Then, using the words you have selected, fill in the blank spaces in the story.

Now you've created your own hilarious MAD LIBS® game!

TOUR OF MONSTRO CITY

ADJECTIVE _____

PLURAL NOUN _____

VERB _____

NOUN _____

PLURAL NOUN _____

OCCUPATION _____

NOUN _____

PLURAL NOUN _____

PLURAL NOUN _____

PART OF THE BODY _____

PLURAL NOUN _____

PLURAL NOUN _____

ARTICLE OF CLOTHING _____

NOUN _____

VERB ENDING IN "ING" _____

NOUN _____

MAD LIBS®
TOUR OF MONSTRO CITY

Welcome to the _____ place we call home! There are so
                      ADJECTIVE

many _____ to see and places to _____ in Monstro
      PLURAL NOUN   VERB

City. You can grab a delicious _____ at the Gross-ery Store,
                                 NOUN

or trade in old _____ at Dodgy Dealz. See if you can get
              PLURAL NOUN

past the _____ at the Underground Disco, or go to
        OCCUPATION

Colorama to change the color of your _____. For you
                                    NOUN

cultured _____, how about a visit to the Googenheim Art
     PLURAL NOUN

Gallery, where you can spend the afternoon looking at pictures of

_____? Got a green _____? Plant some
PLURAL NOUN   PART OF THE BODY

seeds in your garden and see if you can attract some _____!
                                                      PLURAL NOUN

Who doesn't enjoy dressing up in new _____? Buy a new
                                      PLURAL NOUN

_____ for your Moshi so he or she can be the
ARTICLE OF CLOTHING

_____ of the walk on Ooh La Lane. With such hustling and
NOUN

_____ activity, maybe we should change our slogan
VERB ENDING IN "ING"

to "The _____ that Never Sleeps!"
           NOUN

MAD LIBS® is fun to play with friends, but you can also play it by yourself! To begin with, DO NOT look at the story on the page below. Fill in the blanks on this page with the words called for. Then, using the words you have selected, fill in the blank spaces in the story.

Now you've created your own hilarious MAD LIBS® game!

WHO AM I?

NOUN _____

PART OF THE BODY (PLURAL) _____

TYPE OF LIQUID _____

PART OF THE BODY _____

ADJECTIVE _____

ADJECTIVE _____

VERB ENDING IN "ING" _____

NOUN _____

ADJECTIVE _____

NOUN _____

VERB ENDING IN "ING" _____

NOUN _____

CELEBRITY _____

MAD LIBS
WHO AM I?

Du-u-ude . . . I'm not the handsomest _____ on the beach.
                                          NOUN
One of my _____ is missing, and there is usually
          PART OF THE BODY (PLURAL)
some _____ dripping out of my _____.
     TYPE OF LIQUID   PART OF THE BODY
But once you get to know me, you'll see I'm way _____.
                                                    ADJECTIVE
I'm kind of a/an _____ patchwork thingamajig. I dig
                   ADJECTIVE
_____, so I'm always super stoked for a trip to
 VERB ENDING IN "ING"
the Underground _____. I also like to rock out to some
                     NOUN
_____ jams with my air-_____. If you ever feel like
 ADJECTIVE   NOUN
_____, I'm totally your _____! Who am I?
 VERB ENDING IN "ING"   NOUN

Answer: (Here's a hint—it's either Zommer or _____ . . . Still
                                                 CELEBRITY
can't guess? It's Zommer! Tough one—they're so much alike!)

MAD LIBS® is fun to play with friends, but you can also play it by yourself! To begin with, DO NOT look at the story on the page below. Fill in the blanks on this page with the words called for. Then, using the words you have selected, fill in the blank spaces in the story.

Now you've created your own hilarious MAD LIBS® game!

THE *DAILY GROWL*

ADJECTIVE _____

A PLACE _____

VERB _____

ADJECTIVE _____

VERB _____

NOUN _____

NOUN _____

PART OF THE BODY (PLURAL) _____

PERSON IN ROOM _____

TYPE OF FOOD _____

PLURAL NOUN _____

SAME PLURAL NOUN _____

NOUN _____

NUMBER _____

NOUN _____

ADJECTIVE _____

ADVERB _____

MAD LIBS®
THE DAILY GROWL

"_____ morning, citizens of (the) _____. Roary
   ADJECTIVE   A PLACE
Scrawl here with all the news that's fit to _____. I've been
                                              VERB
hearing some _____ noises coming from the Observatory
              ADJECTIVE
lately, so I went over there to _____. I spotted Tamara Tesla
                                 VERB
inventing a new kind of _____! At least I think so, anyway. It
                          NOUN
was either that or a/an _____—I couldn't really tell because
                          NOUN
my _____ aren't so good! In other news, I headed
    PART OF THE BODY (PLURAL)
over to visit my good buddy, _____. His/her house is
                              PERSON IN ROOM
rockin' the _____ wallpaper and she's/he's got loads of
             TYPE OF FOOD
_____! I have no idea why a Moshi would need all those
PLURAL NOUN
_____, but as they say, 'One Moshi's trash is another
SAME PLURAL NOUN
Moshi's _____.' Finally, for _____ days only, the
         NOUN   NUMBER
rare Ultimate _____ can be yours if you visit the Bizarre
               NOUN
Bazaar. This _____ item is on sale for a limited time only, so
              ADJECTIVE
be sure to get one as _____ as possible!"
                       ADVERB

MAD LIBS® is fun to play with friends, but you can also play it by yourself! To begin with, DO NOT look at the story on the page below. Fill in the blanks on this page with the words called for. Then, using the words you have selected, fill in the blank spaces in the story.

Now you've created your own hilarious MAD LIBS® game!

GOOPERSTAR INTERVIEW WITH ZACK BINSPIN

NOUN _____

VERB _____

NOUN _____

EXCLAMATION _____

NOUN _____

NOUN _____

PLURAL NOUN _____

NOUN _____

NOUN _____

PART OF THE BODY (PLURAL) _____

MAD LIBS®
GOOPERSTAR INTERVIEW WITH ZACK BINSPIN

Q: How did you get started in your career?

A: I dreamed of being a singer ever since I was a little _____.
NOUN

My parents say I could _____ before I could talk.
VERB

Q: How did you get your big break?

A: One day I went for a walk on Ooh La Lane, and I was humming a tune called "Raindrops Keep Falling on My _____."
NOUN

Suddenly, I heard a voice say, "_____! You have the voice
EXCLAMATION

of a/an _____!" I turned around and saw Simon Growl! He
NOUN

asked if I wanted to record a/an _____! Of course I said yes.
NOUN

Q: What's your favorite thing about going on tour?

A: I love meeting all my adoring _____, because it's really all
PLURAL NOUN

about them. I may drive a fancy _____ and live in a large
NOUN

_____, but at the end of the day, I sing to touch people's
NOUN

_____.
PART OF THE BODY (PLURAL)

MAD LIBS® is fun to play with friends, but you can also play it by yourself! To begin with, DO NOT look at the story on the page below. Fill in the blanks on this page with the words called for. Then, using the words you have selected, fill in the blank spaces in the story.

Now you've created your own hilarious MAD LIBS® game!

HOW WELL DO YOU KNOW MONSTRO CITY?

NOUN _____

ARTICLE OF CLOTHING _____

COLOR _____

ADJECTIVE _____

VERB _____

NOUN _____

PLURAL NOUN _____

NOUN _____

PLURAL NOUN _____

ADJECTIVE _____

NOUN _____

MAD LIBS®
HOW WELL DO YOU KNOW MONSTRO CITY?

Q: Where do Moshi Members go to change the color of their

_____?
   NOUN

A: Colorama!

Q: If you want to buy a choptastic _____ or a/an
                                          ARTICLE OF CLOTHING

_____ belt for your karate uniform, where do you go?
     COLOR

A: Katsuma Klothes!

Q: Where can you buy _____ gifts for your friends?
                              ADJECTIVE

A: Gift Island!

Q: If you want to visit Elder Furi, you can _____ all the way
                                                      VERB

down the deep, hot _____ to . . .
                          NOUN

A: . . . Super Moshi Headquarters!

Q: Where can you go to test your knowledge of _____, play
                                                        PLURAL NOUN

_____ puzzles, and earn _____ to buy _____
     NOUN   PLURAL NOUN   ADJECTIVE

things for your _____?
                       NOUN

A: Puzzle Palace!

MAD LIBS® is fun to play with friends, but you can also play it by yourself! To begin with, DO NOT look at the story on the page below. Fill in the blanks on this page with the words called for. Then, using the words you have selected, fill in the blank spaces in the story.

Now you've created your own hilarious MAD LIBS® game!

SUPER MOSHI MISSION

PLURAL NOUN _____

NOUN _____

A PLACE _____

ADJECTIVE _____

PLURAL NOUN _____

EXCLAMATION _____

NOUN _____

ADJECTIVE _____

NOUN _____

NOUN _____

ADJECTIVE _____

COLOR _____

NUMBER _____

ADJECTIVE _____

A PLACE _____

NOUN _____

PERSON IN ROOM _____

ADJECTIVE _____

MAD LIBS®
SUPER MOSHI MISSION

Oh my _____! A rare Moshling _____ has been
      PLURAL NOUN   NOUN

stolen from Buster Bumblechops's (the) _____. This looks
                                              A PLACE

like a job for . . . a/an _____ Moshi! To solve this mystery,
                            ADJECTIVE

I will whip out my magnifying glass to search for _____.
                                                              PLURAL NOUN

_____! Here's a torn _____—a/an _____
EXCLAMATION   NOUN   ADJECTIVE

clue if I ever saw one. Aha! What's this? A strange _____—
                                                                         NOUN

another valuable clue—and here on the floor I see muddy

_____-prints. Well, it's pretty obvious what happened based
  NOUN

on these clues. The thief, who was wearing _____ boots,
                                                  ADJECTIVE

has _____ hair, and weighs approximately _____
       COLOR   NUMBER

pounds, entered the scene at precisely ten o'clock last night. He stole

the item and fled to his _____ hideout in (the) _____,
                           ADJECTIVE   A PLACE

thinking he'd gotten away with the perfect _____. Little does
                                                   NOUN

he know that I, Super Moshi sidekick _____, will stop at
                                        PERSON IN ROOM

nothing until he is brought to justice, and Monstro City is

_____ once again!
ADJECTIVE

MAD LIBS® is fun to play with friends, but you can also play it by yourself! To begin with, DO NOT look at the story on the page below. Fill in the blanks on this page with the words called for. Then, using the words you have selected, fill in the blank spaces in the story.

Now you've created your own hilarious MAD LIBS® game!

RECIPE FOR SLOP

ADJECTIVE _____

NOUN _____

ADJECTIVE _____

VERB _____

NOUN _____

ADVERB _____

ADJECTIVE _____

NUMBER _____

NOUN _____

TYPE OF LIQUID _____

ADJECTIVE _____

ADJECTIVE _____

VERB _____

NOUN _____

NOUN _____

MAD LIBS®
RECIPE FOR SLOP

Slop is by far the most _____ food you can give your Moshi
                              ADJECTIVE
Monster if you want to improve his or her _____. Sure, you can
                                                 NOUN
buy it at the Gross-ery Store, but here is a/an _____ recipe for
                                                   ADJECTIVE
all you sentimental types who want to _____ it from scratch:
                                            VERB

1. Start with a/an _____ base. Stir _____ on
                         NOUN   ADVERB
   low heat until it's _____.
                          ADJECTIVE

2. Add _____ cups of sugar, one _____,
            NUMBER   NOUN
   finely chopped, and a few drops of _____.
                                         TYPE OF LIQUID

3. Use a blender to puree it all into a/an _____, porridge-
                                                ADJECTIVE
   like, slurpity glurp, and cover tightly so all the _____
                                                          ADJECTIVE
   flavors _____ together.
              VERB

4. After two hours, give it a taste test. If it tastes like a sweet
   _____, it's done! Add a/an _____ for garnish,
        NOUN   NOUN
   and serve!

MAD LIBS® is fun to play with friends, but you can also play it by yourself! To begin with, DO NOT look at the story on the page below. Fill in the blanks on this page with the words called for. Then, using the words you have selected, fill in the blank spaces in the story.

Now you've created your own hilarious MAD LIBS® game!

FAN CLUB MEETING

PERSON IN ROOM _____

A PLACE _____

ADJECTIVE _____

PERSON IN ROOM _____

COLOR _____

ANIMAL _____

NUMBER _____

PERSON IN ROOM _____

NOUN _____

PART OF THE BODY _____

ARTICLE OF CLOTHING _____

PERSON IN ROOM _____

NOUN _____

ADJECTIVE _____

NOUN _____

VERB _____

PERSON IN ROOM _____

NOUN _____

MAD LIBS®
FAN CLUB MEETING

I do hereby call the one hundredth meeting of the Moshi Monsters fan club to order. Thanks to _____, who decorated (the)
PERSON IN ROOM
_____ with _____ goo in honor of our one
A PLACE   ADJECTIVE
hundredth meeting, and to _____, who brought the
PERSON IN ROOM
Essence of _____ and _____ soda. We've finally met
COLOR   ANIMAL
our fund-raising goal of _____ Rox. _____
NUMBER   PERSON IN ROOM
led our chapter in _____ sales, so now we can finally buy
NOUN
that _____ chair we've been wanting for the lounge.
PART OF THE BODY
Regarding the design of our new fan-club _____,
ARTICLE OF CLOTHING
_____ has created two designs. One features a slimy
PERSON IN ROOM
_____ and the other shows a/an _____ Moshling.
NOUN   ADJECTIVE
You can vote for your favorite at the end of today's _____.
NOUN
Finally, the winner of this month's "_____ like a
VERB
Moshi" contest is _____! Congratulations! Your
PERSON IN ROOM
artful _____ will appear in the Googenheim, to be
NOUN
enjoyed by one and all!

MAD LIBS® is fun to play with friends, but you can also play it by yourself! To begin with, DO NOT look at the story on the page below. Fill in the blanks on this page with the words called for. Then, using the words you have selected, fill in the blank spaces in the story.

Now you've created your own hilarious MAD LIBS® game!

FAN LETTER

A PLACE _____

ADJECTIVE _____

NUMBER _____

ADJECTIVE _____

ARTICLE OF CLOTHING _____

ADJECTIVE _____

PLURAL NOUN _____

NOUN _____

NUMBER _____

PART OF THE BODY _____

ADJECTIVE _____

NOUN _____

TYPE OF FOOD _____

VERB ENDING IN "ING" _____

PERSON IN ROOM _____

MAD LIBS
FAN LETTER

Dear Blingo,

Greetings from (the) _____, my hometown. I just want to
                                         A PLACE
tell you that I think you are the most _____ Moshling, and I
                                                                 ADJECTIVE
am your number-_____ fan. I love your _____ gold
                             NUMBER   ADJECTIVE
necklace, sleek leather _____, and _____
                                        ARTICLE OF CLOTHING   ADJECTIVE
shades. Where do you buy all your _____? Main Street?
                                                               PLURAL NOUN
My favorite song is "Diggin' Ya _____." I watch the
                                                              NOUN
video _____ times a day, and I know all the words by
              NUMBER
_____. Is it fun to make _____ videos?
     PART OF THE BODY   ADJECTIVE
You can e-mail me at BLInGoFaN@_____.com to tell
                                                                         NOUN
me the answers. Please also tell me what your favorite flavor of
_____ is.
    TYPE OF FOOD
Your _____ fan,
            VERB ENDING IN "ING"

_____
    PERSON IN ROOM

MAD LIBS® is fun to play with friends, but you can also play it by yourself! To begin with, DO NOT look at the story on the page below. Fill in the blanks on this page with the words called for. Then, using the words you have selected, fill in the blank spaces in the story.

Now you've created your own hilarious MAD LIBS® game!

GOOD ENOUGH
FOR THE GOOGENHEIM

ADJECTIVE _____

NOUN _____

A PLACE _____

NUMBER _____

NOUN _____

VERB _____

NOUN _____

ADJECTIVE _____

TYPE OF LIQUID _____

VERB _____

NOUN _____

PLURAL NOUN _____

NOUN _____

PART OF THE BODY _____

PLURAL NOUN _____

ADJECTIVE _____

PLURAL NOUN _____

OCCUPATION _____

MAD LIBS®
GOOD ENOUGH FOR THE GOOGENHEIM

Follow these simple instructions to create _____ artwork for
                                            ADJECTIVE
the Googenheim!

1. Start by drawing a picture of a giant _____ in
                                                  NOUN

   (the) _____. Use at least _____ different colors.
         A PLACE   NUMBER

2. Crumple your drawing into a/an _____ and
                                          NOUN

   _____ on it with your feet. Pick up the _____
        VERB   NOUN

   and spread it out on a/an _____ surface.
                               ADJECTIVE

3. Paint with good-quality _____ so the colors
                              TYPE OF LIQUID

   don't _____ together. Have fun and unleash your
            VERB

   inner _____. How do you feel inside—like a million
          NOUN

   _____? Like a/an _____ out of water? Sick to your
   PLURAL NOUN   NOUN

   _____? Let it show in your artwork!
   PART OF THE BODY

4. Make more and more _____ until you have a complete
                       PLURAL NOUN

   collection. Then give your collection a/an _____
                                                  ADJECTIVE

   name, such as "The Many _____ of Me." Now
                            PLURAL NOUN

   you're a real _____!
                  OCCUPATION

MAD LIBS® is fun to play with friends, but you can also play it by yourself! To begin with, DO NOT look at the story on the page below. Fill in the blanks on this page with the words called for. Then, using the words you have selected, fill in the blank spaces in the story.

Now you've created your own hilarious MAD LIBS® game!

MOSHI GEAR!

NOUN _____

PLURAL NOUN _____

PLURAL NOUN _____

NOUN _____

NOUN _____

ADJECTIVE _____

ADJECTIVE _____

PLURAL NOUN _____

NOUN _____

NUMBER _____

EXCLAMATION _____

A PLACE _____

ADJECTIVE _____

NOUN _____

PLURAL NOUN _____

PLURAL NOUN _____

SAME PLURAL NOUN _____

ADJECTIVE _____

MAD LIBS®
MOSHI GEAR!

Welcome to the _____ Shop! We have the largest supply of
                    NOUN
Moshi Monster _____ anywhere in town! Check out our
                PLURAL NOUN
range of plush _____, _____ figures, top-of-
                  PLURAL NOUN   NOUN
the-_____ stickers, books, posters, and more! Check out
       NOUN
this _____ new arrival: a book called *The Moshi Monsters*
       ADJECTIVE
_____ *Guidebook*. Wow your friends with your extensive
 ADJECTIVE
knowledge of Moshi _____! How about this fine-art collectible
                     PLURAL NOUN
_____? It's _____-of-a-kind and guaranteed to make
   NOUN   NUMBER
your friends say, "_____!" How would you like to go to
                     EXCLAMATION
(the) _____ every day wearing this _____ Moshling
        A PLACE   ADJECTIVE
backpack? And you can pack your lunch in this stylish _____,
                                                        NOUN
featuring Luvli and colorful _____. Do you like trading
                              PLURAL NOUN
_____? Well, we have all the Moshi Monsters trading
 PLURAL NOUN
_____—you can collect 'em all! So come on down and
 SAME PLURAL NOUN
pick up some _____ Moshi gear today!
                ADJECTIVE

MAD LIBS® is fun to play with friends, but you can also play it by yourself! To begin with, DO NOT look at the story on the page below. Fill in the blanks on this page with the words called for. Then, using the words you have selected, fill in the blank spaces in the story.

Now you've created your own hilarious MAD LIBS® game!

DEFINITIONS

ADJECTIVE _____

PLURAL NOUN _____

ADJECTIVE _____

A PLACE _____

PLURAL NOUN _____

PLURAL NOUN _____

NOUN _____

NUMBER _____

ADJECTIVE _____

NOUN _____

NOUN _____

ADVERB _____

VERB _____

NOUN _____

ANIMAL _____

MAD LIBS® DEFINITIONS

Here are a few _____ definitions to help you understand the
                    ADJECTIVE
Moshi universe.

1. *Moshling*: Moshlings are little _____ for your
                                         PLURAL NOUN
monsters that are found in _____ places around (the)
                                  ADJECTIVE
_____. They really love _____.
   A PLACE   PLURAL NOUN

2. *Rox*: This is Moshi money that you can use to buy items like food,
drinks, and _____ for your Moshi Monster, as well as
               PLURAL NOUN
items to decorate your monster's _____.
                                         NOUN

3. *Leveling Up*: Each monster begins at Level _____, and in
                                                       NUMBER
order to move up they need to be happy and they need XP. When
they finally move up a level, they do a/an _____ dance
                                                    ADJECTIVE
and you receive a/an _____ as a reward!
                            NOUN

4. *XP*: This refers to _____ Points. _____ playing
                              NOUN   ADVERB
Moshi Monsters will earn you the maximum allowable amount,
so make sure to _____ with your _____ every
                       VERB   NOUN
day to keep him or her as happy as a/an _____!
                                                  ANIMAL

From MOSHI MONSTERS MAD LIBS® • © 2014 Mind Candy Ltd. Moshi Monsters is a trademark of Mind Candy Ltd. All rights reserved.
Published by Price Stern Sloan, an imprint of Penguin Group (USA) LLC, 345 Hudson Street, New York, NY 10014.

MAD LIBS® is fun to play with friends, but you can also play it by yourself! To begin with, DO NOT look at the story on the page below. Fill in the blanks on this page with the words called for. Then, using the words you have selected, fill in the blank spaces in the story.

Now you've created your own hilarious MAD LIBS® game!

MOSHI HOLIDAYS

ADJECTIVE _____

PLURAL NOUN _____

A PLACE _____

ADJECTIVE _____

TYPE OF FOOD _____

ADJECTIVE _____

ADJECTIVE _____

VERB _____

ANIMAL _____

NOUN _____

OCCUPATION _____

VERB _____

VERB _____

PLURAL NOUN _____

MAD LIBS®
MOSHI HOLIDAYS

Moshi Monsters celebrate Pranksgiving, Roy G. Biv Day, Twistmas, and Growly Grub Day. I wish our holidays were as _____ as
ADJECTIVE
these, so I've invented a few new ones:

1. "Slimy _____ Day": We can celebrate by decorating
   PLURAL NOUN

   (the) _____ with slime and other _____
   A PLACE   ADJECTIVE

   party favors.

2. I declare the second Tuesday in August to be "_____
   TYPE OF FOOD

   Day," where we can eat, drink, and be _____!
                                          ADJECTIVE

3. The _____ holidays "_____ like a/an
        ADJECTIVE   VERB

   _____ Day" and "National _____
   ANIMAL   NOUN

   Day" should take place in August, right after "Talk like a/an

   _____ Day."
   OCCUPATION

4. Let's make the last day of every month "Twist and _____
                                                       VERB

   Day." We'll all laugh and _____ in the streets!
                              VERB

I love holidays—the music, the parties, the _____. But
                                              PLURAL NOUN
mostly I love missing school!

MAD LIBS® is fun to play with friends, but you can also play it by yourself! To begin with, DO NOT look at the story on the page below. Fill in the blanks on this page with the words called for. Then, using the words you have selected, fill in the blank spaces in the story.

Now you've created your own hilarious MAD LIBS® game!

THANK-YOU LETTERS

ADJECTIVE _____

ADJECTIVE _____

NOUN _____

ADVERB _____

TYPE OF FOOD _____

ADVERB _____

NOUN _____

ADJECTIVE _____

NOUN _____

ADJECTIVE _____

ADJECTIVE _____

NOUN _____

NOUN _____

VERB ENDING IN "ING" _____

ADVERB _____

MAD LIBS®
THANK-YOU LETTERS

Dear Luvli: I'm writing this _____ note to thank you
                              ADJECTIVE
for the _____ postcard you sent me from _____
         ADJECTIVE   NOUN
Island. Thanks for thinking of me so _____. You are as sweet
                                        ADVERB
as _____. Yours _____: Poppet
   TYPE OF FOOD   ADVERB

Dear Zommer: Thanks for this . . . umm . . . well, I'm not sure what it
is. A/An _____? Well, whatever it is, it sure is _____!
          NOUN   ADJECTIVE
I'm going to put it in my room next to the _____ you got
                                              NOUN
me for Twistmas! _____ regards: Furi
                   ADJECTIVE

Dear Diavlo: Thank you so much for the "Get _____ soon"
                                              ADJECTIVE
message. It really brightened my _____. I was feeling a little
                                    NOUN
under the _____, but now I feel like _____ at
             NOUN   VERB ENDING IN "ING"
the Underground Disco! Wanna join me?

See you _____: Katsuma
          ADVERB

From MOSHI MONSTERS MAD LIBS® • © 2014 Mind Candy Ltd. Moshi Monsters is a trademark of Mind Candy Ltd. All rights reserved.
Published by Price Stern Sloan, an imprint of Penguin Group (USA) LLC, 345 Hudson Street, New York, NY 10014.

MAD LIBS® is fun to play with friends, but you can also play it by yourself! To begin with, DO NOT look at the story on the page below. Fill in the blanks on this page with the words called for. Then, using the words you have selected, fill in the blank spaces in the story.

Now you've created your own hilarious MAD LIBS® game!

NEW CLOTHES

VERB _____

PLURAL NOUN _____

ADJECTIVE _____

NOUN _____

PLURAL NOUN _____

NOUN _____

PART OF THE BODY _____

PLURAL NOUN _____

VERB ENDING IN "ING" _____

NOUN _____

NOUN _____

ADJECTIVE _____

VERB _____

PLURAL NOUN _____

PART OF THE BODY _____

MAD LIBS
NEW CLOTHES

Moshi Monsters dress to _____ and love to try on all the
                         VERB
latest _____ at the Monstro City Marketplace. If you're
       PLURAL NOUN
looking for things that are pink and _____, go to Poppet's
                                     ADJECTIVE
Closet. But if you want something small and _____-colored,
                                             NOUN
try Diavlo's Duds. If you've got a lot of _____ to spend, head
                                          PLURAL NOUN
over to Furi Fashion, where even the smallest _____ can cost
                                              NOUN
you an arm and a/an _____. But if you're saving your
                    PART OF THE BODY
_____ for a rainy day, I recommend _____
PLURAL NOUN   VERB ENDING IN "ING"
somewhere else. Did you adopt a Luvli? Take her to Luvli Looks,
where a flying _____ will help you find all you need.
               NOUN
Katsuma Klothes is the destination if you are shopping for your
_____. In one of their many _____ kung fu outfits,
NOUN   ADJECTIVE
your monster will _____ in style. Finally, if you want new
                  VERB
_____ for your Zommer, head over to Zommer's Drop Dead
PLURAL NOUN
Threads. Maybe pick him up a spare _____ while you're
                                   PART OF THE BODY
there, too!

From MOSHI MONSTERS MAD LIBS® • © 2014 Mind Candy Ltd. Moshi Monsters is a trademark of Mind Candy Ltd. All rights reserved.
Published by Price Stern Sloan, an imprint of Penguin Group (USA) LLC, 345 Hudson Street, New York, NY 10014.

MAD LIBS® is fun to play with friends, but you can also play it by yourself! To begin with, DO NOT look at the story on the page below. Fill in the blanks on this page with the words called for. Then, using the words you have selected, fill in the blank spaces in the story.

Now you've created your own hilarious MAD LIBS® game!

HAPPINESS

ADJECTIVE _____

NOUN _____

PLURAL NOUN _____

NUMBER _____

NOUN _____

PART OF THE BODY _____

VERB ENDING IN "ING" _____

PLURAL NOUN _____

CELEBRITY _____

PLURAL NOUN _____

ADJECTIVE _____

PLURAL NOUN _____

ADVERB _____

COLOR _____

PART OF THE BODY _____

NOUN _____

NOUN _____

VERB _____

MAD LIBS®
HAPPINESS

There is no _____ secret to making your Moshi Monster as
         ADJECTIVE
happy as a/an _____. It's simple—every monster needs food,
                 NOUN
fun, and _____. Make sure you feed it _____ times
          PLURAL NOUN   NUMBER
a day, and tickle it by moving the _____ around its
                                       NOUN
_____. Take your monster out _____
PART OF THE BODY   VERB ENDING IN "ING"
and decorate its room with lots of _____ and posters of
                                    PLURAL NOUN
_____. Play with new _____, do _____
  CELEBRITY   PLURAL NOUN   ADJECTIVE
puzzles, and go out to visit your _____. If you don't
                                   PLURAL NOUN
do these things for a long time, your monster will get angry and
_____ start seeing _____. Sometimes Diavlo gets
  ADVERB   COLOR
so frustrated that smoke comes out of his _____!
                                          PART OF THE BODY
Zommer will throw his _____ across the room, and even
                         NOUN
Poppet can scream like a wild _____! So look out, and
                                  NOUN
remember to play, eat, tickle, and _____ with your Moshi
                                       VERB
every day!

MAD LIBS® is fun to play with friends, but you can also play it by yourself! To begin with, DO NOT look at the story on the page below. Fill in the blanks on this page with the words called for. Then, using the words you have selected, fill in the blank spaces in the story.

Now you've created your own hilarious MAD LIBS® game!

CAP'N BUCK

A PLACE _____

ADJECTIVE _____

PLURAL NOUN _____

NOUN _____

ADJECTIVE _____

NOUN _____

NOUN _____

PLURAL NOUN _____

PLURAL NOUN _____

PART OF THE BODY _____

NOUN _____

NUMBER _____

ADJECTIVE _____

MAD LIBS®
CAP'N BUCK

Ahoy, maties! It's great to be back in (the) _____ after a/an
                                         A PLACE
_____ time out at sea. I been to a place 'ere the waterfalls be
ADJECTIVE
spillin' o'er with _____. It's called Bubblebath Bay, and it
                    PLURAL NOUN
smells as fresh as a/an _____. Blargh! I like seafarin'
                             NOUN
adventures, but there be nothin' like the _____ smells o'
                                           ADJECTIVE
home. Now I be tryin' t' smell like a sea _____ again by
                                                NOUN
rubbin' m'self all over with a/an _____! Anyway, I brought
                                      NOUN
back some pirate's booty for all you wee _____. I'm not
                                            PLURAL NOUN
gonna spill the _____ on what it is—mystery and intrigue be
                 PLURAL NOUN
what's good fer business . . . Okay, ye twisted my _____.
                                                    PART OF THE BODY
I brought ye a/an _____ machine. I'll be in town for only
                      NOUN
_____ days, so get it while the gettin's _____!
   NUMBER   ADJECTIVE

MAD LIBS® is fun to play with friends, but you can also play it by yourself! To begin with, DO NOT look at the story on the page below. Fill in the blanks on this page with the words called for. Then, using the words you have selected, fill in the blank spaces in the story.

Now you've created your own hilarious MAD LIBS® game!

DECORATING MY MOSHI MONSTER'S ROOM

A PLACE _____

ADJECTIVE _____

PLURAL NOUN _____

ADJECTIVE _____

ADJECTIVE _____

PLURAL NOUN _____

PLURAL NOUN _____

PLURAL NOUN _____

NOUN _____

NOUN _____

ADJECTIVE _____

NOUN _____

NOUN _____

ADVERB _____

NOUN _____

PLURAL NOUN _____

NOUN _____

PLURAL NOUN _____

MAD LIBS®
DECORATING MY MOSHI MONSTER'S ROOM

Hi, kids! Tyra Fangs here, reporting from (the) _____ on
                                              A PLACE

how to make your room as _____ as it can be! Monsters
                          ADJECTIVE

luuuurrrve to entertain _____, so get your room looking
                         PLURAL NOUN

fangtastic by purchasing some _____ items from the Monstro
                               ADJECTIVE

City shops. Yukea has everything for the _____ monster's
                                          ADJECTIVE

room, from slimy _____ to fuzzy _____. Choose
                  PLURAL NOUN   PLURAL NOUN

your wallpaper and then accent it with _____. Every Moshi
                                         PLURAL NOUN

Monster's room needs a/an _____ poster and _____
                            NOUN   NOUN

ball, and you can find these at the Bizarre Bazaar. If you visit Horrods,

you can find some truly _____ items, such as a lava
                         ADJECTIVE

_____ and a shimmering snaggletooth _____.
    NOUN   NOUN

Display these _____ in your room, so visitors will know that
                ADVERB

you are one classy _____. And if you really want to create an
                     NOUN

inviting space for _____, buy an animated _____
                    PLURAL NOUN   NOUN

chair. All the best _____ have one!
                     PLURAL NOUN

MAD LIBS® is fun to play with friends, but you can also play it by yourself! To begin with, DO NOT look at the story on the page below. Fill in the blanks on this page with the words called for. Then, using the words you have selected, fill in the blank spaces in the story.

Now you've created your own hilarious MAD LIBS® game!

MENU FOR
TWISTMAS BANQUET

PLURAL NOUN _____

NOUN _____

NUMBER _____

ADJECTIVE _____

NOUN _____

NOUN _____

NOUN _____

A PLACE _____

NOUN _____

TYPE OF FOOD _____

NOUN _____

NOUN _____

PLURAL NOUN _____

NOUN _____

ADJECTIVE _____

PART OF THE BODY _____

MAD LIBS®
MENU FOR TWISTMAS BANQUET

Thank you, fellow Moshi _____, for attending this year's
                         PLURAL NOUN
formal _____ in honor of Twistmas Day. I am Snozzle
        NOUN
Wobbleson, and I'm here to present the menu for tonight's banquet.
Our _____-course dinner features a/an _____
     NUMBER   ADJECTIVE
appetizer of _____ surprise with _____ sauce.
              NOUN   NOUN
Next, we'll cleanse the palate with some _____-flavored
                                          NOUN
sorbet, imported from (the) _____. Then we'll partake in a/an
                             A PLACE
_____ salad. Please inform your waiter if you desire fresh
 NOUN
ground _____ sprinkled over the top. The main course is
        TYPE OF FOOD
roasted _____ with a/an _____ stuffing and braised
         NOUN   NOUN
_____ on the side, and the dessert is _____ upside-
 PLURAL NOUN   NOUN
down cake. These dishes may not sound _____ to you, but
                                       ADJECTIVE
to Moshi Monsters—Zommer in particular—they are positively
_____-watering.
 PART OF THE BODY

MAD LIBS® is fun to play with friends, but you can also play it by yourself! To begin with, DO NOT look at the story on the page below. Fill in the blanks on this page with the words called for. Then, using the words you have selected, fill in the blank spaces in the story.

Now you've created your own hilarious MAD LIBS® game!

C.L.O.N.C.

ADJECTIVE _____

ADJECTIVE _____

VERB ENDING IN "ING" _____

PLURAL NOUN _____

TYPE OF FOOD _____

NOUN _____

NOUN _____

ADJECTIVE _____

PLURAL NOUN _____

PART OF THE BODY _____

PART OF THE BODY (PLURAL) _____

OCCUPATION _____

PLURAL NOUN _____

MAD LIBS®
C.L.O.N.C.

As you navigate the Moshi universe, you must keep your Moshi

Monster _____ at all times. Beware of Dr. Strangeglove,
         ADJECTIVE

Monstro City's most _____ criminal mastermind. He turns
                         ADJECTIVE

Moshlings into Glumps with his _____ machine. Don't
                                VERB ENDING IN "ING"

cross _____ with Sweet Tooth, either. That sugary psycho will
       PLURAL NOUN

offer you _____ and it will make you fall asleep! Frau Now
           TYPE OF FOOD

BrownKau is wanted in connection with _____ theft, and
                                           NOUN

Robo Quacks once stole Baby Rox's _____! Monstro City is
                                        NOUN

a/an _____ place with lots of friendly _____, but
      ADJECTIVE   PLURAL NOUN

keep your _____ up and your _____
          PART OF THE BODY   PART OF THE BODY (PLURAL)

open. If you see any suspicious activity, please report it to the nearest

_____. It's up to you to keep Monstro City safe from
   OCCUPATION

_____!
  PLURAL NOUN

From MOSHI MONSTERS MAD LIBS® • © 2014 Mind Candy Ltd. Moshi Monsters is a trademark of Mind Candy Ltd. All rights reserved.
Published by Price Stern Sloan, an imprint of Penguin Group (USA) LLC, 345 Hudson Street, New York, NY 10014.

MAD LIBS® is fun to play with friends, but you can also play it by yourself! To begin with, DO NOT look at the story on the page below. Fill in the blanks on this page with the words called for. Then, using the words you have selected, fill in the blank spaces in the story.

Now you've created your own hilarious MAD LIBS® game!

UNDERGROUND DISCO

PLURAL NOUN _____

VERB ENDING IN "ING" _____

NOUN _____

VERB ENDING IN "ING" _____

OCCUPATION _____

NOUN _____

SILLY WORD _____

PART OF THE BODY (PLURAL) _____

VERB ENDING IN "ING" _____

NOUN _____

NUMBER _____

NOUN _____

EXCLAMATION _____

VERB (PAST TENSE) _____

ADVERB _____

NOUN _____

MAD LIBS®
UNDERGROUND DISCO

What's up, _____? This is Poppet. Yesterday I had so much
           PLURAL NOUN

fun rockin' and _____ at the Underground Disco!
                 VERB ENDING IN "ING"

All my friends were there, cutting a/an _____ to the latest
                                              NOUN

Moshi tunes. We started by _____ to the beat of
                             VERB ENDING IN "ING"

"The _____ Will See You Now!" and the "Sweet Tooth
       OCCUPATION

_____." Then we swayed to "Do the _____" and
     NOUN   SILLY WORD

"Head Over _____." When we finished dancing,
           PART OF THE BODY (PLURAL)

I entered a/an _____ contest, just for fun. Tyra Fangs
                VERB ENDING IN "ING"

said my singing reminded her of a/an _____! Roary Scrawl
                                          NOUN

gave me _____ out of ten, and Simon Growl said I had all
          NUMBER

the potential of a budding _____. I said, "_____!"
                               NOUN   EXCLAMATION

and felt like I could have _____ all night, but instead I
                            VERB (PAST TENSE)

skipped _____ all the way home to bed. Ah, the Underground
         ADVERB

Disco, where we all get to feel like _____-stars.
                                          NOUN

This book is published by

PSS!

PRICE STERN SLOAN

whose other splendid titles include
such literary classics as

Ad Lib Mad Libs®	Mad About Animals Mad Libs®
Best of Mad Libs®	Mad Libs® for President
Camp Daze Mad Libs®	Mad Libs® from Outer Space
Christmas Carol Mad Libs®	Mad Libs® in Love
Christmas Fun Mad Libs®	Mad Libs® on the Road
Cool Mad Libs®	Mad Mad Mad Mad Mad Libs®
Dance Mania Mad Libs®	Monster Mad Libs®
Dear Valentine Letters Mad Libs®	More Best of Mad Libs®
Diva Girl Mad Libs®	Night of the Living Mad Libs®
Dude, Where's My Mad Libs®	Ninjas Mad Libs®
Easter Eggstravaganza Mad Libs®	Off-the-Wall Mad Libs®
Escape from Detention Mad Libs®	The Original #1 Mad Libs®
Family Tree Mad Libs®	P. S. I Love Mad Libs®
Fun in the Sun Mad Libs®	Peace, Love, and Mad Libs®
Girls Just Wanna Have Mad Libs®	Pirates Mad Libs®
Gobble Gobble Mad Libs®	Prime-Time Mad Libs®
Goofy Mad Libs®	Rock 'n' Roll Mad Libs®
Grab Bag Mad Libs®	Slam Dunk Mad Libs®
Graduation Mad Libs®	Sleepover Party Mad Libs®
Grand Slam Mad Libs®	Son of Mad Libs®
Hanukkah Mad Libs®	Sooper Dooper Mad Libs®
Happily Ever Mad Libs®	Spooky Mad Libs®
Happy Birthday Mad Libs®	Spy Mad Libs®
Haunted Mad Libs®	Straight "A" Mad Libs®
Holly, Jolly Mad Libs®	Totally Pink Mad Libs®
Hot Off the Presses Mad Libs®	Undead Mad Libs®
Kid Libs Mad Libs®	Upside Down Mad Libs®
Letters from Camp Mad Libs®	Vacation Fun Mad Libs®
Letters to Mom & Dad Mad Libs®	Winter Games Mad Libs®

You've Got Mad Libs®

and many, many more!

Mad Libs® are available wherever books are sold.